Unrequited

GINA MARIE CRAIG

To order additional copies of this book, contact:
Xlibris
844-714-8691
www.Xlibris.com
Orders@Xlibris.com

ISBN: Softcover   978-1-6698-5114-1
         EBook   978-1-6698-5113-4

Print information available on the last page

Rev. date: 10/25/2022

For: Sofia Rose

This book was created for my daughter to help her
with the heartbreak and experience of love.

Table of Contents

Come Back to Me

Please tell me where we went wrong.

All I do is think of you when I hear my favorite song.

I want you more than you know.

I can't seem to let go.

It hurts so bad inside.

You really took me for a ride.

Our attraction was so intense, but I know fleeting.

Can we have another meeting?

I'm holding out hope you will come back to plead your case.

The connection we have is too tight to erase.

Exposed

I feel so ashamed and sick inside

Exposing my naked body for everyone to see.

You told me "Come on baby it's just for me".

But you lied and it took away my self-respect.

How could I be so naïve to think you wouldn't betray me?

I allowed my addictions with lust to control me.

Fortunately, I took my power back because my reputation and dignity are still intact.

I know you must be battling your own demons that I can't do anything about.

2

3

Forbidden Love

Why do I feel such an uncontrollable desire?

It is like playing with fire.

I want you so bad that it hurts me so.

I can't seem to let you go.

How Dare You

Do you think you got the best of me?

You just couldn't let things be!

If I had only listened to my head not my heart.

Nothing would've gone anywhere from the start.

It really doesn't matter, because in the end I know one thing.

You can't destroy a good human being.

You Hurt Me Deeply

Do you know how much you hurt me?

I cry myself to sleep at night, how can this be?

You thought because you could pull my strings.

I would do anything.

Guess what, I am getting over it.

You will never know what hit.

Because in the end your hold only lasted so long.

I am slowly picking up the pieces and getting strong!

Unrequited

How did I end up in this dark place?

Something I don't like to face.

It haunts me every day.

Knowing there's no other way.

If things could be different, I would make it so.

Instead I'm haunted by your memory and can't let this feeling go.

Printed in the United States
by Baker & Taylor Publisher Services

I Want to be Whole Again

Sitting here reflecting on my thoughts.

Of all the past wrongs and where I missed my shots.

To be a better person is who I want to be.

Seeking approval of others who will never understand me.

That elusive quest for the kind of happiness I don't believe exists.

Please make me whole inside as I look for those missing parts of my heart.

All I want is true unconditional understanding and love.

Something or someone that can put me above.

All the other things in this world where there is just not enough.

It's such a pipe dream to want such things.

Why is it that I have these feelings?

I Want You in My Life

I want you in my life even though it's not right.

Too many obstacles in our way.

My heart aches for you every day.

My desire for you grows stronger in every way.

Undeniable passion that exits.

Please take me away from all of this

I'm Done Crying Over You

How can you be so cruel?

Stomping on my heart while you broke me apart.

Is this a game with no rules?

I must have been a fool to trust the likes of you.

You enjoy my pain.

What is it you must gain?

I want to take back that day you ran away.

So, I could tell you how I really feel.

For that you could not appeal.

My tears of sadness have turned to gladness.

Knowing deep inside you suffer as much as I.

I saw the way you looked at me.

You knew I could set you free from your life of misery.

I'm Not Over You

Alone in my room crying over you.

Realizing we were through!

The memories of the excitement I felt when I first saw you.

That won't go away no matter what I do.

11

Just One Night

If I could have you for just one night.

Would you want to be mine?

How bad do you want me?

We can't deny how bad we want to feel that desire in our bodies and souls.

Take my breath away.

I'll be forever yours

Like a Drug

You're like a drug to me

Getting into my system the first day you looked at me

I wanted you from the first moment I saw you.

It's the forbidden fruit that I wasn't trying to find

Unable to get you out of my mind.

The longer you are gone the more I withdrawal.

Please fulfill my fantasies and we can have it all.

My Heart Has Turned Cold

The desire I once had for you has turned into regret.

I let you in my life knowing deep down inside I would get no respect.

My head is spinning around with thoughts of what you said.

Sometimes I wish that you were dead.

It would be easier that way.

You cowardly disappeared without an explanation.

I guess I deserved it for I fell to your temptation.

If you ever return, I will tell you where to go.

I never again want to feel that low.

My Heart's Desire

I wasn't trying to fall for you when you came into my life.

But there was something about you I couldn't deny.

You touched a part of me that I didn't realize I had inside.

The part that makes me come alive

Obsession

How did you do this to me?

Making me smile this joyfully?

I have not been able to think of anything but you.

Unable to do the things I used to.

That which filled me up with joy.

Don't you be so coy!

I'm obsessing about the thought of your touch.

I want it so much.

I'm missing your smiling face and the way it makes my heart race.

Tell me you feel the same.

Or I will feel so much shame.

For I can't go one more day with the possibility of knowing you don't want it that way.

I need to have you in my life.

Without you this world cuts like a knife.

SHAME

Trying to hold back my tears alone in my bed.

Contemplating everything you said.

I ignored all the red flags that were waved.

If only I had behaved.

Knowing the danger of the situation.

Completely disregarding my reputation.

I got taken by your looks and charm.

You only wanted to do me harm.

Twin Flame

I know what we felt was love at first sight.

Try as hard as we can to deny it.

We touched a part of each other like no one before.

The attraction between us was magnetic.

There's no other person that has ever made my heart race this fast.

You come to me in my dreams.

I'm trying to forget you but impossible it seems.